DETERMINED FAITH

BY

MIKE KEYES, SR.

WORD & SPIRIT
PUBLISHING

Determined Faith
Copyright © 2020 by Mike Keyes, Sr.
ISBN: 978-1-949106-42-8

Published by Word and Spirit Publishing
P.O. Box 701403
Tulsa, Oklahoma 74170
wordandspiritpublishing.com

CONTENTS

PART ONE

UNDERSTANDING THE PROCESS

And He said, "The Kingdom of God is as if a man should scatter seed on the ground, and should sleep by night and rise by day, and the seed should sprout and grow, he himself does not know how. For the earth yields crops by itself: first the blade, then the head, after that the full grain in the head. But when the grain ripens, immediately he puts in the sickle, because the harvest has come."

—MARK 4:26-29

CHAPTER 1

You Can't Please God without Faith

But without faith it is impossible to please Him, for he who comes to God must believe that He is, and that He is a rewarder of those who diligently seek Him.

—HEBREWS 11:6

If we have a desire to please God, we must develop our faith in Him and His Word. This verse says it is *impossible* to please the Lord without faith. It didn't say it is hard, it said it is impossible. Every believer is charged with the responsibility to develop a productive faith-life, if they want to be pleasing to God. If we love God, we are obligated to learn how to live by faith. The more we commit to this, the more our faith will grow (2 Thessalonians 1:3).

Jesus gave important instructions regarding the life of faith.

> *"So Jesus answered and said to them, 'Have faith in God. For assuredly, I say to you, whoever says to this mountain, "Be removed and be cast into the sea," and does not doubt in his heart, but believes that those things he says will be done, he will have whatever he says. Therefore I say to you, whatever things you ask when you pray, believe that you receive them, and you will have them,'"* (Mark 11:22-24).

These verses show four things we must know and apply to have faith that pleases God. First, Jesus tells us to have faith in God, because all things are possible when we do (Mark 9:23). Second, He shows us there are two ways faith can be exercised. Third, He tells us faith is released and put to work by the words we speak. Fourth, He instructs us to speak to the mountain, which represents the problem we're using faith to remove.

In Mark 11:12-21, the disciples were stunned over what they saw Jesus do. He had cursed a fig tree, and within a matter of hours, the tree had died from the roots. In the natural that's not possible, but faith in God can do the impossible. The entire eleventh chapter of Hebrews declares this. How did Jesus curse the fig tree? He spoke to it, and this is what He instructs us to do. Whoever *says* to this mountain, believing that those things he *says* will be done, he will have whatever he *says*. This shows us the importance of choosing our words carefully, if we're to have faith like God.

Mark chapter 11, verse 23, talks about *exercising our authority* in the name of Jesus. Because of what Jesus accomplished on the cross, there are some things we don't need to ask for in prayer, because God has already declared they belong to us in Christ. As believers, we just need to use our authority to change things when necessary, in order for the will of God to come to pass in our lives.

In many cases, we don't need to pray to God about the "mountain" standing in our way. Just like our Lord said, we speak to it in the name of Jesus, *expecting it to move*. Verse 24 talks about *praying the prayer of faith* in the name of Jesus. When we do need to ask God for help, we pray prayers of faith. That means we believe we receive what we prayed for *at the time we prayed*, even when we don't immediately see anything that indicates the prayer was heard and answered by God. We walk by faith, *not by sight* (2 Corinthians 5:7). Either way, Jesus promised results when we exercise our faith in God. The more we walk by faith, the stronger in faith we become, and the more pleasing we are to God.

CHAPTER 2

Plant a Mustard Seed

Then He said, "To what shall we liken the Kingdom of God? Or with what parable shall we picture it? It is like a mustard seed which, when it is sown on the ground, is smaller than all the seeds on earth; but when it is sown, it grows up and becomes greater than all herbs, and shoots out large branches, so that the birds of the air may nest under its shade."

—MARK 4:30-32

Jesus compares the Kingdom of God to the planting of a mustard seed. His emphasis here is not just the fact we must plant a seed, but the size of the seed when planted. In addition, in the verses preceding these, Jesus tells us that everything in the Kingdom of God operates on the laws of sowing and reaping (Mark 4:26-29). Everything means *everything*. Study and learn the principles of farming, and we'll understand how God operates on Earth in response to our faith.

When we put all these verses together from Mark chapter 4, it teaches us six important things. First, we have to have seeds before we can plant them. Second, unplanted seeds can never produce a harvest. Third, the size of the seed doesn't determine the size of the harvest. Concerning the Kingdom of God, seeds can *appear* to be very small when planted, but will eventually produce a harvest much, much larger. Fourth, planted seeds must be watered and fertilized to grow. Fifth, planted seeds need to be protected until the harvest. Finally, seed time and harvest time is not the same time. Patience must be exercised in between. We don't plant on Monday and get our harvest on Tuesday. That's not how things work with God. Through faith *and* patience, we inherit the promises of God (Hebrews 6:12).

The Bible is a book of words about words. The Kingdom of God is governed by spoken words. By our words we are justified, and by our words we are condemned (Matthew 12:34-37). Death and life are in the power of the tongue (Proverbs 18:21). *The words we speak are the seeds we sow.* Remember Mark 11:22-24. God responds to the words we speak (Daniel 10:12). Spoken words are planted—either as faith seeds or fear seeds. Words of faith empower God to move on our behalf. Words of fear empower the devil against us—to steal, kill, and destroy (John 10:10). Which kind of seed we plant is up to us. Our words determine our harvest. What we say determines what we see. Faith is the evidence of things *not seen* (Hebrews 11:1). *If we change what we say, what we say will change what we see.*

Once we understand how God's kingdom operates on Earth, we know our options are two-fold when planting seeds of faith to overcome satanic obstacles in our way. We use our authority as ambassadors of Christ, speaking to mountains to move them (2 Corinthians 5:20), or concerning things promised in God's Word, we believe we receive when we pray the prayer of faith (Matthew 21:22). Either way, *we must say what we believe to plant our faith seeds*. Once planted, more words of faith need to be spoken to water, fertilize, and protect our seeds until the promised harvest comes. All of this takes time, which is why determination is necessary if patience is to have its perfect work.

CHAPTER 3

Let Patience Have
Its Perfect Work

*My brethren, count it all joy when you fall
into various trials, knowing that the testing
of your faith produces patience. But let
patience have its perfect work, that you may
be perfect and complete, lacking nothing.*

—JAMES 1:2-4

If we compare the life of faith to the business
of farmers planting crops, we know there is a
time period between seed time and harvest time.
For earthly farmers, that growing period for the
kind of seed sown is known and established,
consistent from one planting season to the next.
But in God's kingdom, the growing period
varies, depending upon an individual's level of

faith, surrounding circumstances, and the degree of demonic resistance. Therefore, the need for patience is critical. There are three cooperating powers that work with our faith during times of testing or trial. First, there is *patience*. Second, there is *experience*. And third, there is *hope*. (Romans 5:1-5 KJV)

Faith is the evidence of things *not seen* (Hebrews 11:1). Every time we exercise our authority or pray the prayer of faith, the enemy will try and prevent us from receiving what we want or need. Our faith is a shield that fends off all the fiery darts of the enemy (Ephesians 6:16), but we must stand our ground for as long as it takes, because those fiery darts will keep on coming! That's why we must clearly understand the spiritual planting process, as outlined in Mark 11:22-24. For as long as it takes, we must couple our words of faith with patience, believing we *already have* what we've declared or prayed for in Jesus' name. This demands determination, an attitude that many Christians fail to exhibit, which is why they fail to receive. With each faith victory we gain more experience, which protects our hope when fighting future good fights of faith (1 Timothy 6:12).

James also tells us to count it all joy when our faith is tested by the enemy, because the joy of the Lord is our strength (Nehemiah 8:10). This is not happiness. Happiness is external and carnal. Anyone can be happy, including sinners. Joy is a fruit of the recreated human spirit (Galatians 5:22), and it only comes from God. When consistently applied, joy enables us to stand patiently without wavering in our confessions of faith, until victory has been won. If we're truly in faith, joy should be the outward expression of our inner convictions. That's why it's called the *joy of faith* (Philippians 1:25). The world should *see* our joy when our seeds are in the growing season! Joy demonstrates our faith. It will *let* patience have its perfect work, so we'll be perfect and complete, lacking nothing. It's the strength from heaven that always brings in the crop!

We count it *all joy* when our seeds our being threatened. All means all the time. We should *continue to rejoice*, even when we're grieved and weighed down through multiple demonic attacks and trials. This proves our faith is *genuine,* and in God's sight, genuine faith that has been tested in the fires of spiritual combat is more precious than gold. This makes our faith walk even more honorable, glorious, and praiseworthy when Jesus returns (1 Peter 1:6-7). Faith is defined as substance and evidence (Hebrews 11:1). It is not a feeling. It is a noun. Believing is a verb. *Believing is the act of releasing our faith and putting it to work.*

When we're believing we should be rejoicing (1 Peter 1:8)! They go together. And it's in the rejoicing we find the strength to patiently endure without wavering, no matter what the devil does to try and dig up our seeds! When we are determined to keep believing, without yet seeing what we are using faith for, the joy of our faith becomes so overwhelming words can't describe it—it's inexpressible!

Knowing these things, we can begin to praise the Lord joyfully, knowing that as we *continue* to patiently stand, we'll receive the results our faith was applied to produce (Ephesians 6:13).

CHAPTER 4

Patience Protects Faith

Cast not away therefore your confidence, which hath great recompence of reward. For ye have need of patience, that, after ye have done the will of God, ye might receive the promise.

—HEBREWS 10:35-36 KJV

Joyful patience protects our faith, and along with experience and hope, keeps it active and productive during the growing season. Proverbs 28:20-22 tells us that faithful men abound with blessings, but those who hasten to receive will be punished. Faithful men exercise patience once their faith seeds are planted, knowing that sooner or later they'll receive whatever they have declared or requested from God. We are joyful while we wait, because we know God's harvest is guaranteed (Mark 11:22-24 and Luke 8:15). The unfaithful are they who "hasten" to receive what they need from God. They plant their faith seeds with the words they speak, but lack the patience to remain joyful under pressure, to do what's necessary to guard their seeds until the harvest comes.

Once a farmer plants his crop, he leaves it in the ground to begin the growing process. Because it's planted in the ground, he can't see the seeds germinate and start to grow, but he has faith to believe they do. He doesn't run out into the field every week in a panic, pulling up the seeds to see if they've taken root and started to grow, because he knows that will kill the seeds and destroy the crop. That's exactly what they who "hasten" to receive are doing. Their impatience allows the enemy to pull up and destroy the seeds that they've planted. They give up too quickly when under attack, because they lack the determination to stand, and having done all to do, continue to stand (Ephesians 6:13)!

Proverbs 21:5 tells us that hasty people will *surely* come to poverty. That means failure is guaranteed for the impatient. To be hasty is to be impatient, and impatient people are easy targets for the devil. Demonic attacks will surely come against us once we declare our faith and plant our seeds. Satan will never just let us have what God promises without putting up a fight. He will try to apply as much pressure as possible, hoping we will cave in to fear, doubt, and unbelief, which if we do, means we'll quit watering, weeding, and fertilizing our seeds with joyful praise. Past experiences of faith victories will be forgotten, and hope for our current fight of faith will be extinguished.

Revelation 12:11 says we can overcome attacks of the enemy by the blood of Jesus, and *the word of our testimony*. That means patience must be vocal. It must be aggressively declared out loud. Faith *comes* by consistently hearing the Word of God (Romans 10:17), and faith is *protected* by consistently hearing the Word of God as well. Verbally, believers must rehearse past victories to combat present temptations. We

take evil thoughts captive by speaking to them
(2 Corinthians 10:3-5). In addition, deferred
hope makes the heart sick (Proverbs 13:12).
This is hope that has been put off and laid
aside. Deferred hope means the mental picture
of victory has been replaced with thoughts of
defeat and a lost crop. That creates a sick heart,
which will never be strong enough to resist all
those fiery darts from the enemy.

Our faith must be coupled with a steely
determination to get what God promises in His
Word. Without it, we'll have very little chance
of remaining joyfully patient in faith until our
harvest comes in. We'll lay down our faith and
quit confessing the promises we stood upon at
the time we planted our faith seeds. And that
impatience will only serve to torment us going
forward, because impatient believers are always
thinking and talking about what they want but
never get—and will never get from the Lord!

CHAPTER 5

Diligence and Determination

*And we desire that each one of you show the
same diligence to the full assurance of hope
until the end, that you do not become sluggish, but imitate those who through faith
and patience inherit the promises.*

—HEBREWS 6:11-12

The Bible instructs us not to become *sluggish*, and show *the same diligence until
the end*. To be "sluggish" is to be lazy, lethar-
gic, and apathetic. The "same diligence" is the
same determination that others have used to stay
steadfast from the day the seed was planted, to
the day the harvest came up. The "full assurance of hope" is our protected mental picture of

victory. It's the power of scriptural imagination. The "end" is the actual victory we plant our faith seeds to get. Determination is the attitude that refuses to tolerate laziness, lethargy, or apathy and triumphantly takes us from the beginning to the end in every fight of faith, so we can "lay hold" of the promises Jesus died to make available to us (1 Timothy 6:12).

When the disciples burst out of the upper room on the day of Pentecost, they delivered the first recorded salvation message (see Acts chapter 2). The fires of international evangelism began to burn, first in Jerusalem, then Judea, Samaria, and to the ends of the earth (Acts 1:8). As expected, and as Jesus had forewarned, the devil did his best to apply intense pressure against the early church, endeavoring to destroy it before it became a worldwide juggernaut for God.

To stand against this onslaught, the early church leaders exhorted the saints to find their steadfast strength in the Word of God, exactly as we must do today. But since the New Testament books hadn't yet been written to read and study, all they had to refer to were the Old Testament books. Nothing else was available. The four gospels hadn't yet been written. The epistles hadn't yet been written. The New Testament wasn't completed and widely distributed until many years later, so to strengthen and encourage the believers as they faced "fiery trials" of persecution (1 Peter 4:12-16), the Lord instructed them to find Old Testament examples of those who through *faith and patience,* inherited the promises of God. They were told to imitate heroes of faith back then, as we are to imitate them today (see Hebrews chapter 11).

Thank God for the New Testament, which has completed the revelation of God's plan for man. And thank God for all the additional testimonies from New Testament saints like Paul, whom we can now study and draw strength from. But if God knew the Old Testament examples of faith and patience were good enough for His early church to successfully fight their good fights of faith, we can certainly find sufficient instruction and guidance from those same brethren today. We need to carefully contemplate the challenges people of the Old Testament faced when they decided to trust God in faith for things promised in the Word of God. Let's look at examples found in the Old Testament, to see how important it is to couple a determined attitude with the decision to patiently wait upon God for promised answers.

We must remember these people were no different than you and I, and faced many obstacles that, without determination, would've caused them to abandon their faith long before their harvest had come. This passage from Hebrews tells us to *imitate* the people who received what they believed God for back in their day, so we can show the same diligence in full assurance of hope until the end in our day. Let's find out what they overcame to get what they wanted from God. Let's see how critical their determination was in holding their ground in faith, all the way to the finish line of victory.

PART TWO

IMITATE THEM!

And we desire that each one of you show the same diligence to the full assurance of hope until the end, that you do not become sluggish, but imitate those who through faith and patience inherit the promises.

—HEBREWS 6:11-12

CHAPTER 6

Two Blind Men

When Jesus departed from there, two blind men followed Him, crying out and saying, "Son of David, have mercy on us!" And when He had come into the house, the blind men came to Him. And Jesus said to them, "Do you believe that I am able to do this?" They said to Him, "Yes, Lord." Then He touched their eyes, saying, "According to your faith let it be to you." And their eyes were opened. And Jesus sternly warned them, saying, "See that no one knows it." But when they had departed, they spread the news about Him in all that country.

—MATTHEW 9:27-31

Two blind men *followed* Jesus. Blind men can't see. How difficult would it be for men who can't see to try and follow someone who can? Both men wanted healing, because they were crying out for the Lord to have mercy on them when they finally stood before Him. But notice it says after Jesus came into the house, the blind men *came to Him*. Only God knows how far they had to go to catch up and come to Jesus face-to-face, but whether it was short or long in terms of distance, I'm sure it was tempting to quit, give up and stumble home, as blind as ever.

Don't you know that as Jesus was walking along at a normal pace (with multitudes of people walking with Him and all around Him), the two blind men were falling further and further behind? There's no indication here that anyone was helping them or escorting them. If you can't appreciate what they had to overcome, blindfold yourself and try following someone walking down the street, and see if you can keep up! These two blind men wouldn't give up. They kept on going for however long it took, until finally they caught up with Jesus in that house.

When they finally got to the Lord to ask for their miracle healing, Jesus had one question for them: "Do you *believe* I'm able to do this? They said they did and they proved it—not because they said so standing there, but because of their dogged determination displayed in refusing to give up until they got to the place where Jesus could minister to them. Jesus told them it was *according to their faith* they received their sight. That faith was coupled with determination. They fell farther behind with every step Jesus took on the road that day, and it seemed more and more impossible that they'd ever be healed. But they refused to be deterred, because they had the determination to keep going for however long it would take until they had the miracle they desired. They decided to couple their faith with patience, and their patience with determination.

? *ASK YOURSELF.* When the chance of a miracle healing is walking faster and further away with each step taken, would you or I have the raw determination to continue chasing after the Lord, groping along in total darkness like these two did, without any assistance from anyone? *Think about it*.

CHAPTER 7

The Canaanite Mother

Then Jesus went out from there and departed to the region of Tyre and Sidon. And behold, a woman of Canaan came from that region and cried out to Him, saying, "Have mercy on me, O Lord, Son of David! My daughter is severely demon-possessed." But He answered her not a word. And His disciples came and urged Him, saying, "Send her away, for she cries out after us." But He answered and said, "I was not sent except to the lost sheep of the house of Israel." Then she came and worshiped Him, saying, "Lord, help me!" But He answered and said, "It is not good to take the children's bread and throw it to the little dogs." And she said, "Yes, Lord, yet even the little dogs eat the crumbs which fall from their masters' table." Then Jesus answered and said to her, "O woman, great is your faith! Let it be to you as you desire." And her daughter was healed from that very hour.

—MATTHEW 15:21-28

A mother's love for her children is something precious to behold. In this passage, that love compelled this woman to seek out healing for her demon-possessed daughter. She came to Jesus, crying out for His mercy, asking Him to cast that devil out and heal her daughter. One problem though—she wasn't a Jew. She was a Gentile. The law forbade Jews to interact with Gentiles, and both our Lord and His disciples knew this. That's why initially He ignored her. Basically, Jesus was answering her without answering her. His silence declared it wouldn't be right to take what was offered to Jews (healing), and give it to heathen (Gentiles) like her. But she kept following Jesus and wouldn't go away, and that irritated the disciples to the point they publicly urged the Lord to get rid of her.

When Jesus finally spoke up, He didn't speak to her directly, but to His disciples. To explain his perceived rudeness, He reminded them all that He was sent to the Jews, not to the Gentiles. Because He knew she could hear what He was saying, the Lord was informing her by what He was telling them. She was being told she didn't qualify for His time or attention, so that's why He refused to respond to her. But the Word says she *still came and worshipped Him,* pleading her case repeatedly.

What an attitude! Qualified or not, this woman was determined to get an answer out of Jesus. But when Jesus finally turns and speaks directly to her, His response is not what she's looking for! When explaining His refusal to even address her situation, Jesus calls her a dog and says it's not right to give dogs the food meant for children eating at the table. At that time the Jews commonly referred to Gentiles as "dogs"—a derogatory term for people unworthy of God's time or attention. By using such terminology, the Lord was telling this Canaanite woman it was wrong to give to people like her and her daughter the healing power that had been promised only to the Jews. *Ouch!*

Look at the perceived insults she took on the chin! First, Jesus ignored her as if she wasn't even there. Then, while she's standing there, she hears the disciples urging Jesus to get rid of this uninvited irritant, as she's becoming an embarrassing public spectacle. Next, while she's within earshot to hear it, Jesus tells the disciples He's not sent to minister to Gentiles like her. But she was determined to forge ahead! She falls before the Lord in worship, again pleading unashamedly for the help her daughter needs. In a moment of excited anticipation, she saw Jesus turn to finally speak with her directly, but His answer is another blow she wasn't expecting. She's called a dog, undeserving of even the leftover scraps from the children's table, making a clear distinction between qualified Jews and unqualified Gentiles like her and her daughter.

But she was *still* not deterred! She comes back with an answer that blesses me every time I read it. She says to Jesus, "Yes, I'm a dog—whatever! Call me what You want Lord, but even dogs like me get to eat crumbs that fall from their owner's table!" Wow! What an answer! She's telling Jesus and anyone else who was close enough to hear, that she's not going anywhere until He does something about her demon-possessed daughter! She doesn't care what the public thinks. She doesn't care what the indignant disciples think. She doesn't even care what Jesus thinks! She's *determined* to get her answer!

And how did the Lord respond? With anger and indignation? Absolutely not! He loved her determination—and so do I! "O woman, *great is your faith!* Let it be for you as you have desired!" The demon was driven out that day, and the mother had a healed daughter to come home to! Without such determined faith, this miracle would never have happened.

? *ASK YOURSELF.* Today, if people came to God with legitimate needs and encountered such perceived hostility, 99 percent of them would become highly offended at God, at

Jesus, and at anything having to do with the Gospel. They would storm off in a huff, never to darken the doors of a church again. Would we be among the 99 percent like that, or the 1 percent like her? Would you or I have this much determination with our faith? How many times was this woman rebuffed? She wouldn't quit. She wouldn't give up. And Jesus loved it! Would you continue to plead your case like she did, until you get what you need from God? *Think about it*.

CHAPTER 8

The Sick Mountain Climbers

Jesus departed from there, skirted the Sea of Galilee, and went up on the mountain and sat down there. Then great multitudes came to Him, having with them the lame, blind, mute, maimed, and many others; and they laid them down at Jesus' feet, and He healed them. So the multitude marveled when they saw the mute speaking, the maimed made whole, the lame walking, and the blind seeing; and they glorified the God of Israel.

—MATTHEW 15:29-31

Where is Jesus in these verses? Sitting down, *at the top of the mountain.* It then says great multitudes came to Him. Where did they have to go to come to Him? To the top of the mountain. How many were coming to Jesus? Not just a multitude, or a great multitude, but great *multitudes!* That means the crowds numbered in the thousands, maybe even more. What kind of people were in these great multitudes, climbing the mountain to come to Him? Were they all just healthy people wanting to hear more of our Lord's wonderful teachings? No! They were there because they wanted Jesus to heal them or their sick friends and relatives. Were these minor ailments to be healed, like headaches, colds, ingrown toenails, skin rashes, and the like? Hardly. These mountain climbers coming to Jesus included *lame, blind, mute, maimed, and many others,* which means there were innumerable cases of serious, incurable, terminal, hopeless sicknesses, handicaps, and diseases included in the crowds.

Whether it be for ministry or personal recreation, have you ever done any serious hiking or uphill climbing, on hills or mountains? I have for both, and I can tell you that even if you're in good condition physically, it's still a hardy workout! Its challenging. Your lungs hurt. Your legs feel like they're burning. Your feet often get blistered. Your knees ache. Your clothes are soaked in sweat. Well, these people climbing up the mountain to get to Jesus weren't Olympic athletes in training, and for sure, the sick and handicapped they were bringing with them weren't either. This was going to be "tough sledding" any way you look at it.

And notice Jesus didn't lift a finger to help. Neither did He send His disciples down the slope to provide any assistance. No, He just sat up there, watching all these people struggle up the mountain with their sick, handicapped friends, neighbors, or relatives. How challenging do you think it would be, even with some assistance, for a blind man to climb a mountain? How about for a mute or deaf person? Or, how about for those who are lame or maimed? Lame means something is wrong and you can't walk right, maybe from birth. Maimed means you've been severely injured and have got damaged or even amputated limbs. It took determined faith for these great multitudes to climb the mountain to get to Jesus.

Once they got to the top, the Bible says they "laid them down" at Jesus' feet, and He healed them. The terminology used in translations like the NKJV suggests the sick and handicapped were gently laid at our Lord's feet. In the Greek however, it indicates chaotic activities from the crowd that were more spontaneous and desperate. The King James Version uses a different word to describe what was happening at the top of the mountain, saying they *cast* the sick down at Jesus' feet. That's much more accurate. In the Greek, that English word "cast" means to *"throw with a quick, sudden motion."* Here is what *Strong's, Vines,* and the King James Version has to say about that word "cast":

> *Strong's:* Grk word *"rhipto"*
> NT:4496 *rhipto* (hrip'-to); a primary verb (perhaps rather akin to the base of NT:4474, through the idea of sudden motion); to fling (properly, with a quick toss, thus differing from NT:906, which

denotes a deliberate hurl; and from *teino* [see in NT:1614], which indicates an extended projection); by qualification, to deposit (as if a load); by extension, to disperse:

KJV – cast (down, out), scatter abroad, throw.

Vine's Expository of NT Words: CAST 2. *rhipto* NT:4496 denotes "to throw with a sudden motion, to jerk, cast forth"; "cast down," Matt 15:30 and 27:5; "thrown down," Luke 4:35; "thrown," 17:2 (KJV "cast"); [rhipteo in Acts 22:23 (KJV "cast off"), of the "casting" off of clothes (in the next sentence ballo No. 1, is used of "casting" dust into the air)]; in 27:19 "cast out," of the tackling of a ship, in v. 29 "let go" (KJV "cast"), of anchors; in Matt 9:36, "scattered," said of sheep. See THROW, SCATTER.

These people weren't carefully laying the sick or handicapped people down—they were literally throwing, hurling, or heaving them down in front of Jesus! Remember, there were *great multitudes* doing this. I've seen this for myself in our crusades in the Philippines. When crowds are desperate and excited simultaneously like this, it's mass hysteria! There is no healing line. There are no "catchers" behind the sick, to catch them in case people fall out under God's power. You just try to control the chaos!

Whenever the Lord ministered to individuals or small groups like the two blind men we looked at earlier, He always made sure they knew that it was *their faith* that produced their miracle healing. He never mentioned their determination or patience in so many words, but the fact they overcame such huge obstacles in each case was proof enough. However, in this case at the top of the mountain, Jesus never specifically commended people for their faith, simply because there were multitudes being healed, one right after another in an atmosphere of pure pandemonium.

It took enormous determination for the crowds to climb the mountain as they did. In addition, once they finally got to the top, they had to exercise even more determination to pick up their handicapped mother or sick grandfather and throw them at Jesus! Mommy and granddaddy had to have that kind of determined faith as well, believing that when they hit the ground at Jesus' feet and bounced back up, they would be healed!

? *ASK YOURSELF.* With all the pain and difficulty that goes with being very sick or extremely handicapped, would you or I have the determination to climb a mountain to get our healing, like these people? And on top of that, would we allow ourselves to be flung down or thrown to the ground by "loving" friends or relatives, as these people were? *Think about it!*

CHAPTER 9

The Roof Destroyers

And again, He entered Capernaum after some days, and it was heard that He was in the house. Immediately many gathered together, so that there was no longer room to receive them, not even near the door. And He preached the word to them. Then they came to Him, bringing a paralytic who was carried by four men. And when they could not come near Him because of the crowd, they uncovered the roof where He was. So when they had broken through, they let down the bed on which the paralytic was lying. When Jesus saw their faith, He said to the paralytic, "Son, your sins are forgiven you." And some of the scribes were sitting there and reasoning in their hearts, "Why does this Man speak blasphemies like this?

Who can forgive sins but God alone?" But immediately, when Jesus perceived in His spirit that they reasoned thus within themselves, He said to them, "Why do you reason about these things in your hearts? Which is easier, to say to the paralytic, 'Your sins are forgiven you,' or to say, 'Arise, take up your bed and walk'? But that you may know that the Son of Man has power on earth to forgive sins" —He said to the paralytic, "I say to you, arise, take up your bed, and go to your house." Immediately he arose, took up the bed, and went out in the presence of them all, so that all were amazed and glorified God, saying, "We never saw anything like this!"

—MARK 2:1-12

In this passage, Jesus was holding a Bible study in Capernaum and there were so many in attendance, no one else could get into the house. As the Lord was teaching, four men arrived with their paralyzed friend, whom they carried on a cot. Their intent was to have Jesus minister a miracle to their friend, because by this time the whole region was talking about the mighty miracles that were taking place in His meetings. But they couldn't get in. The house was jam-packed. People were sitting in the windows and blocking the entrances. At this point, as it would be today, most people would've shrugged their shoulders, turned around and gone home, consoling the paralyzed man and saying they'll try again some other time. But not these guys! They stood outside surveying the situation, determined to find a way in.

They decided the only way was to split up to get the man on the cot up to the roof, where they could then make a big hole, and lower him into the Bible study so Jesus could minister to him. They presented this idea to their paralyzed friend on the cot, and all five of them agreed to this plan! Two of the four would climb up first, while the other two looked for ways to secure the paralyzed man to the cot. Then two from the top and two from the bottom would work to carefully raise the cot up onto the roof. When that was accomplished, all four of them would begin working on the roof itself, so they could make a hole large enough to lower the cot into the living room where Jesus was teaching.

Sounds like a great plan but for this to happen they faced several major obstacles. Remember, they weren't prepared for any of this. They expected to show up and walk right in the front door. First, they didn't have any climbing tools or equipment like hammers, ropes, pulleys, pinions, carabineers, and so forth. Second, the man on the cot was *paralyzed*, which means he couldn't move. They would have to secure him to the cot and keep it balanced so he didn't slide off as they were trying to lift him up to the roof. What would happen if they failed to do that and the cot tipped or flipped over and he goes sliding off? He was paralyzed, so he would be unable to break his fall. In short, he could be severely injured or even killed. Third, even if they could get the guy up onto the roof in one piece, how were they going to open the roof? Once again, they weren't expecting this. They weren't professional wall climbers *or* roof repairmen! They didn't show up because the homeowner scheduled a roof repair service call, as employees working for *Ezekiel's Roofing Company,* specializing in roof destruction, repair, and resurfacing, with the motto, *"You scratch – we patch!"* No!

The NKJV says they "uncovered" the roof and "broke through" so they could lower the cot. That's a very accurate description of what they were doing. Roofs today are much different than in those days. Back then they were made with straw and other similar materials, compressed with mud or dirt that formed a hard, flat layer when dry. So, how would they uncover and break through? By using their bare hands, because that's all they had to work with. Maybe they gathered a few rocks to help, but nothing specifically designed for the task at hand. Scratching, clawing, pounding, and stomping on the roof, they kept at it until finally they broke through, tearing up and smashing clumps of dried mud and straw to make a big hole. And fourth, *this was not their house!* The homeowner was no doubt inside, hosting Jesus and His entourage, listening to His teachings. He had no idea five total strangers were planning to climb up the side of his house and destroy his roof! And the five total strangers didn't care! They were determined to do what needed to be done—no matter what anyone thought about it, including the homeowner! Picture the scene in your mind.

As Jesus was teaching, the homeowner could hear all kinds of voices and commotion up on his roof. He couldn't get out onto the street to see what all the fuss was about, because all the doors and windows were packed with people. He heard the sound of scratching, pounding, and people kicking and shouting, and more and more dust, bits of straw, and dried mud start falling into his living room! People were coughing, rubbing their eyes, brushing dust and debris off their clothing and out of their hair, no doubt upset because all this commotion was disrupting their Bible study with Jesus.

The homeowner must have been wondering, *what in the world is going on up there?* Finally, along with the whole crowd inside, he saw a small opening in his ceiling, with hands ripping, clawing, and tearing away, until at last there was a big hole in his roof! No doubt the house was filled with dust in the air, and piles of roof debris all over the floor. When the air cleared and he looked up, he saw four total strangers waving and saying "hello!" They lowered the cot carrying a paralyzed man he doesn't know—right through his brand new skylight!

And here's the point to see above all else. The Bible says that when Jesus *saw their faith,* He began to minister forgiveness first, and healing second. We've already seen from scriptures that we plant our seeds of faith by saying what we believe, before we have what we're using faith for. But for that harvest to come up, as it did in this story, we might have to do things we never expected or anticipated—things many might consider extreme. We might have to go beyond the "ordinary," the "predictable," or the "socially acceptable."

Like with Jesus that day, this never bothers God, so why should it bother us? As far as we can tell from this story, while the men were destroying the homeowner's roof, Jesus never tried to stop them. He just let them continue, just like when He was watching without assisting the sick people climbing up the mountain for healing in Matthew chapter 15, or the two blind men trying to find Jesus for healing in Matthew chapter 9. He never said a word in protest over what these five men did to demonstrate such raw faith and determination. People being people, I suspect the homeowner was quite upset with what had just happened to his roof. I mean, he didn't have homeowner's insurance to fall back on, did he? But as all of this was happening, I can imagine that Jesus just put a calming hand on the man's shoulder, to give him reassurance that everything would be alright, because it always is when we let God take care of us.

? *ASK YOURSELF:* Would you be that determined to overcome obstacles like these if you needed a miracle like this man? Would I? *Think about it.*

CHAPTER 10

The Man Who Would Not Be Silent

Now they came to Jericho. As He went out of Jericho with His disciples and a great multitude, blind Bartimaeus, the son of Timaeus, sat by the road begging. And when he heard that it was Jesus of Nazareth, he began to cry out and say, "Jesus, Son of David, have mercy on me!" Then many warned him to be quiet; but he cried out all the more, "Son of David, have mercy on me!" So Jesus stood still and commanded him to be called. Then they called the blind man, saying to him, "Be of good cheer. Rise, He is calling you." And throwing aside his garment, he rose and came to Jesus. So Jesus answered and said to him, "What do you want Me to do for you?" The blind man said to Him,

"Rabboni, that I may receive my sight."
Then Jesus said to him, "Go your way; your
faith has made you well." And immediately
he received his sight and followed Jesus on
the road.

—MARK 10:46-52

Here we see a blind man named Bartimaeus, sitting and begging by the side of the road. He hears the noise of a great crowd passing by, so he inquires to find out what's going on. When he's told that Jesus of Nazareth is passing by, he gets excited. Everybody's been talking about Jesus and all the miracles He performs, including many blind people like him being healed. No doubt he's been hoping to have the opportunity to meet Jesus and get healed himself, but alas, as a blind beggar along the road on the outskirts of Jericho day after day, he probably thought his chances were slim to none. But wait! *He's here!*

When he starts shouting out for Jesus to have mercy on him for healing, the Bible says many warned him to be quiet. Not just a few told him to shut up—*many* were doing so. What did he do? He began shouting louder and louder! He wasn't going to let the voices in the crowd deter him from raising his own voice in faith to God. They weren't just telling him nicely to be quiet, they were *warning* him! To warn someone means they should be wary because there is danger lurking nearby, and that's what was happening to Bartimaeus. He was being told that if he didn't close his mouth, bad things would happen to him.

But the more he was warned to shut up, the louder he shouted! What an example of determined faith! Pay attention to what happened next, because this is what determined faith will do for us. Jesus *stood still,* and commanded they bring Bartimaeus to Him. When we refuse to be intimidated by all the hypocrites, critics, God-haters, and ignorant Christians out there, and raise our voices to God in faith, He stands still! That means He's blessed by how we're standing our ground in faith, no matter how many people the devil recruits to try and shut us up. We have His attention.

Remember seed time and harvest time—and the time in between. That's when Satan will go to work to rip up our faith seeds, and destroy any hope of a supernatural harvest. He uses whatever or whoever he can to do this. Bartimaeus was unceremoniously told to shut up or bad things would start happening to him. But he *ignored* all the ignorant noise, and pressed in until Jesus stopped and called him forth. And if ever there was a biblical illustration of the hypocrisy of religion and humanity in general, we see it in this story. Once Jesus stopped and commanded this shouting beggar to be brought to him, the *same people* who moments before were telling him to shut up began patting him on the back, helping him up, and telling him to be happy that Jesus was calling for him! You've no doubt heard of "Reality TV?" Well, this is *Religious Reality TV* at its hypocritical finest!

Let us all learn from this story. When it comes time to shout out our faith to God, the devil and his puppets on Earth will always step up to try and stop us. We must *never* let them intimidate or silence us. Follow in the footsteps of Bartimaeus. To get the answers we want, we need to do exactly what the blind beggar did. We declare our need and believe God will meet that need. The more we're told to shut up, the more we confess the Word to water and protect our seeds of faith. The more we're warned to be quiet, the more we declare our harvest in faith. The more we're pressured to back off on our confessions of faith, the louder we shout in praise to our Almighty God.

The question Jesus asked Bartimaeus that day is the same one He asks us every day. *"What do you want Me to do for you?"* A simple question that we should take at face value. Let's declare our authority and state our requests, expecting the Lord to move in our lives (Isaiah 43:26). And during the growing season, we must ignore all efforts by others to convince us to stop shouting the victory! Jesus told Bartimaeus it was his faith that brought him his miracle healing. But if he had listened to all those telling him to shut up, he would've gone on to live and die as a blind beggar. If I'm Bartimaeus, as the hypocrites were helping me up, bringing me to

Jesus with pats on the back and words of encouragement, I'd be thinking *"yeah, no thanks to you, unbelieving buzzards! Jesus stopped and wants to meet me! If I'd listened to you, I'd still be down on the side of the road, a hapless and blind beggar to the day I die!"*

Let's all be like Bartimaeus that day on the Jericho road. We must tune out all the religious hypocrites, ungodly media, hate-filled unbelievers, and anyone else spewing their venom—conveniently sent our way through electronic correspondence like texts, emails, social media, and the like. We must ignore family members who may be well-meaning, but haven't got a clue. Let's cut off and terminate friendships with so-called "friends" trying to dissuade us from believing God. Let's stay zeroed in on promises we see from God's Word that apply to us, and embrace them without apology. The louder the devil-controlled world shouts against us, the more we shout louder and louder until we get the promised harvest our faith seeds were planted to get.

ASK YOURSELF: Would you or I let a crowd of upset bystanders stop us from crying out publicly for mercy and healing, like Bartimaeus did? In the face of rabid, angry commands to shut up, would we continue shouting louder and louder until we got the Lord's attention? *Think about it!*

CHAPTER 11

The Blind Man Who Found the Pool

Now as Jesus passed by, He saw a man who was blind from birth. And His disciples asked Him, saying, "Rabbi, who sinned, this man or his parents, that he was born blind?" Jesus answered, "Neither this man nor his parents sinned, but that the works of God should be revealed in him. I must work the works of Him who sent Me while it is day; the night is coming when no one can work. As long as I am in the world, I am the light of the world." When He had said these things, He spat on the ground and made clay with the saliva; and He anointed the eyes of the blind man with the clay. And He said to him, "Go, wash in the pool of Siloam" (which is translated, Sent). So he went and washed, and came back seeing.

—JOHN 9:1-7

Remember, the Bible wasn't originally written with chapter and verse markings—they were added centuries later for study purposes. That means originally there was no division between the end of John chapter 8 and the start of John chapter 9. According to John 8:20, Jesus started out having a Bible study in the temple, but by the time we reach the end of the chapter, the Jews were so mad at Him, they were looking to stone the Lord for the sin of blasphemy. Realizing it was time to go, He "hid Himself" and left the temple. The last verse of John chapter 8 tells us Jesus *passed by* the angry crowd with stones in their hands, and the first verse of John chapter 9 says that as He and His disciples passed by, they came upon the man blind from birth. It's important to note our Lord's specific location when this encounter took place.

It was a common misconception back then for people to believe that such handicaps were the result of some sin committed by the afflicted or their parents. That's why His disciples asked who was responsible for committing the sin that caused this man to be born blind. Jesus ignores the question because He knows its erroneous. Instead, He declares that God's works should be revealed in this man. This does not mean that God made the man blind so He could later on heal him. It means that when we encounter such people with issues like these, we have the authority to minister miraculous power to them in the name of Jesus. The healing then brings glory to God—not the sickness itself.

Let's look at the details surrounding this man's miracle. To start with, the man never knew it was Jesus of Nazareth standing in front of him. He was blind, so he couldn't see the Lord or His disciples, and wasn't inside the temple listening to Jesus' teachings just moments before. He could hear all the commotion as Jesus was passing by the stone-throwers, but He wouldn't have known what the ruckus was all about. Oblivious to what's just happened inside the temple, He hears a group of men approaching, stopping in front of him, and then discussing his blindness. He hears one man address a rabbi with a question about the possible reasons for his blindness from birth, and then hears the rabbi's answer. But notice that in this whole verbal exchange, Jesus was never addressed by name. He was addressed only as "Rabbi."

There were many rabbis in Israel, so as far as the blind man was concerned, this was nobody special. Just one of the many rabbis and worshippers who passed him on their way into the temple each day. But after hearing the question about his condition, he heard an answer that he had never heard before! While the blind man was listening, Jesus told the disciples not to focus on the issue of who had sinned, because nobody's sin was the cause for this man's handicap. Instead, He exhorted them to realize that while there was still time, He could shine once again as the Light in a very dark world, by giving glory to God through the healing of this poor soul.

The blind man didn't have a clue as to what was happening, or what was about to happen. He just heard the question and the answer from total strangers. He didn't know the rabbi or any of His friends. He didn't know who sent the rabbi, where He came from, what it meant for this rabbi to be light in the world, or how the works of God would be glorified in Him. He didn't even know what the works of God were.

And as if things weren't already confusing enough, it became even more bizarre! He heard somebody spit on the ground, and a few seconds later, felt cool mud being applied to his eyes. He could feel and smell the mud—he knew what was being applied—but didn't know who was doing this, or why. Then he heard the rabbi's voice, this time speaking directly to him and not to the others. This unknown rabbi tells him to find the pool of Siloam and wash the mud off his eyes. That's it! Nothing more is said or done to him. *Notice this command makes no mention of healing!* Jesus never told the blind man that when he washed the mud off his eyes in that particular pool, he would be miraculously healed. Not at all!

And as the TV commercial will say, *"But wait, there's more!"* How was this man going to find the pool? He was blind. Remember that according to John 9:1, as Jesus passed by, He was coming out of the temple. If you look at a map showing Jerusalem at the time of Christ (many Bibles have such a map at the back of the book), you can see the pool of Siloam was on the other side of the city. It was not like the pool was close to the temple, where this encounter was taking place. No, it was far away. It was not like he could whip out his cellphone, tap on Google Maps and get walking directions to the pool. It's not like he could hop on the #9 bus that made a loop around the city, making a stop at the pool of Siloam. It's not like he had friends or loved ones that could escort him to the pool, either.

This situation was just like the gathering on the mountain we talked about earlier, when Jesus chose to sit and watch many severely crippled and handicapped people struggle up the mountain without offering any assistance. This time He sent this man off to find a pool on the other side of the city, with no help or escort. We don't see Jesus instructing any of His disciples to assist this man in his hunt for the pool. He was just left to find the pool by himself, not having any idea about why he should do it. He was totally on his own!

Don't you know it took a great amount of determined faith to do this? No doubt, as he was making his way across town, he was asking people for directions, but how do you give directions to a man who can't see? Remember, this was a city full of obstacles that people walking around with normal vision didn't have to think about. This blind man had to navigate streets that were nothing more than narrow, winding alleys. They were full of people busy with their daily affairs, coming and going, buying and selling their merchandise. Roman soldiers were stationed throughout the city, keeping the peace. Animals and livestock were everywhere. The noise of the city was deafening.

Think about it. What would you say to such a one if he asked for directions? *Where's the pool of Siloam, you ask? Well, you go down this alley until you hit the wall, then turn right. You'll know you're on the right path if you fall into a big drainage ditch. Climb out and keep going, but watch out for the horse stables. You don't want to get kicked in the head. Then the alley will split and you'll need to bear to the left, but be careful not to stumble over the ox carts, or step in their "cow pies" nearby. Just after the ox carts, there's a new sidewalk café that just opened up last month. Don't trip over their tables and chairs. Once you make it to the Roman guard post, you're getting close, but whatever you do, don't step on their toes or run into them accidentally—they're really touchy about things like that. The last guy that did that was crucified. Make a left at the fruit and veggie stand, and you're there!* Yeah, right!

But wait, there's more! As he was on his quest for the pool, don't you know that people, just being people, were asking questions he had no answer for. Question: Why are you looking for the pool of Siloam, blind man? Answer: Because a rabbi told me to find it and wash this mud off my eyes. Question: What rabbi told you to do this? Answer: I don't know. Question: Did you put that mud on your eyes? Answer: No. Somebody spit on the ground, made mud, and put it on my eyes. I believe it was the rabbi. Question: Why did he do that? Answer: I don't know. Question: What's going to happen when you wash that mud off at the pool? Answer: I don't know. Question: Then why are you doing this? Answer: I don't know. I'm just going to do what he told me to do.

Wow! Talk about faith being the evidence of things *not seen* (Hebrews 11:1). The Bible says when he finally found the pool, he washed and received his miracle. He came back *seeing!* Once he got back to his neighborhood, it wasn't long before he found out the rabbi was "a man called Jesus" (John 9:11). When the stunned crowd asked him where Jesus was, he didn't know! When interrogated by the Pharisees later in John chapter 9, he was kicked out of the synagogue for defending the Lord. His answer to them was classic: *Whether Hs is a sinner or not I do not know. One thing I know: that though I was blind, now I see!* (John 9:26).

? *ASK YOURSELF* You've heard the term "blind faith?" This man literally had blind faith, with a lot of determination to go with it. Do you have this kind of determined faith? Do I? What a miracle of God—but what a set of challenges this man had to overcome to receive it. Without this kind of determination, he would've lived the rest of his life blind, just the way he was when Jesus passed by. *Think about it!*

CHAPTER 12

The Choice Is Yours

I call heaven and earth as witnesses today against you, that I have set before you life and death, blessing and cursing; therefore choose life, that both you and your descendants may live.

— DEUTERONOMY 30:19

John 21:25 tells us that if we tried to list every miracle Jesus did in His three-and-a-half-years of public ministry, the world itself could not contain the books that would be written. This side of heaven, only God knows how many miracles were performed by our Lord, but there are too many to count, that's for sure. Second Timothy 3:16 tells us all scripture was given by inspiration of God. The Bible is the Word of God, not the word of men. Men wrote the words, but the Holy Spirit inspired them to write what they wrote.

It's important to remember that every miraculous healing or deliverance highlighted from scripture in this book was hand-picked by the Spirit of God. Matthew, Mark, Luke, and John didn't decide which miraculous stories they would write about—the Holy Spirit did. He could pick from thousands upon thousands of miraculous testimonies to inspire those four men to write about. *Why* did God want us to read about these stories and not others?

It's because He knew these particular miracle testimonies provided all the information we would need to effectively fight our own good fights of faith today. Through these select stories, the Spirit of God wants us to understand the process of seed time and harvest time, and the choices we must make to bring that process successfully to completion. He wants us to know the necessity of planting our seeds of faith with the words of our mouth. He wants us to know the importance of protecting and fertilizing those seeds during the growing season. He wants us to understand that our natural circumstances can be an intimidating force that can keep us from moving those mountains in front of us—if we let them. He wants us to understand that Satan will do everything he can to throw roadblocks in our way.

Finally, He wants us to realize our free will is the greatest weapon we have from God. Whether our determination is applied against the natural weaknesses we all have, or the lying darts the devil tries to plant in our minds, victory is guaranteed. No matter what difficulties, challenges, obstacles, or hurdles we face as we endeavor to walk by faith and not by sight, we can *choose* to remain steadfast, believe the Word of God, hold our ground and advance under fire from the enemy* (for more on this, read my book *Advancing Under Fire*).

ASK YOURSELF. How would you fare if you faced imposing obstacles or natural impediments like all these people? Every miracle story the Holy Spirit placed within the Bible has one purpose—to show us the common denominator of faith coupled with determination. We must understand our *attitude* during various faith fights is critical to receiving our desired outcome. *"Then Peter opened his mouth and said: 'In truth I perceive that God shows no partiality. But in every nation whoever fears Him and works righteousness is accepted by Him,'"* (Acts 10:35). God is no respecter of persons. We can choose to do what they did and get the same results, because Jesus is the same yesterday, today, and forever (Hebrews 13:8). *Think about it!*

ABOUT THE AUTHOR

Mike Keyes grew up in Ohio and was raised in the Roman Catholic church. In 1973, he graduated from college to become a successful advertising executive and graphic artist. On September 21, 1978, at age twentysix, he was born again and Spirit filled two days later. Immediately, the gifts of the Spirit began working in his life. Through his local church, he began to witness on the streets, in area prisons, and anywhere he could hand out tracts.

In September 1979, Reverend Keyes resigned his job to attend Rhema Bible Training Center in Tulsa, Oklahoma, graduating in May 1980. In September 1980, he traveled to the Philippines with a oneway plane ticket, arriving without knowledge of the language or customs and with no one there to meet him. When he got off that plane to begin his ministry, he had twenty dollars in his pocket, one footlocker containing his Bible, class notes, a few changes of clothing, and the promise of support totaling $250 from no one except his parents and one small church in Toledo, Ohio.

From those humble beginnings and through his faithfulness to the calling of God over the years, the Lord has used Reverend Keyes extensively to reach untold numbers of people in the Philippines and around the world. Always emphasizing outreach to the remote, overlooked, outoftheway villages and towns that no one else has gone to, it is conservatively estimated that since the beginning of his ministry's outreach in 1980, over 750,000 souls have been won to Christ in his nationwide crusades in the Philippines.

Mike Keyes Ministries International (MKMI) is an apostolic ministry that reaches the lost, teaches the Christians and trains the ministers. With a consistent crusade outreach, a church network of hundreds of churches, and the Rhema Bible Training Center, Reverend Keyes and his staff, pastors, graduates and students continue to fulfill the Great Commission wherever he is instructed to go by the Holy Spirit—throughout the Philippines and around the world.

Reverend Keyes is married to a native Filipina, Ethel, and has two children.

OTHER BOOKS BY
MIKE KEYES SR

Advancing Under Fire
ISBN: 978-1-939570-47-5

In today's world there has been a gradual "slide" away from God and the things of God. What was once thought perverse and unthinkable is now thought to be the norm. Churches and ministers are bending over backwards to appease people calling their approach "user friendly" or "seeker friendly" not wishing to "offend" anyone. Advancing Under Fire challenges the Body of Christ to rise up, shed the mistakes and failures of the past and join forces to engage the enemy with the truth of the Gospel.

Divine Peace
ISBN: 978-1-939570-17-8

How can you live above fear and pressure and the frantic pace of life in these perilous times? Divine Peace reveals the principles of knowing and walking in God's peace every day and how to stand strong in the midst of every circumstance with a peace that passes all understanding.

OTHER BOOKS BY
MIKE KEYES SR

Be Strong! Stay Strong!
ISBN: 978-1-939570-00-0

God's perfect will is for every believer
to be triumphant and victorious in life.
Be Strong! Stay Strong! shares seven
spiritual priorities and the importance
of practicing them consistently,
bringing any believer to the place of
superior strength and victory over an
attack of the enemy in these last days.

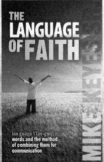

The Language of Faith
ISBN: 978-1-939570-02-4

Have you ever wondered how to com-
municate with God? In *The Language
of Faith*, Mike Keyes, Sr. reveals the
rules that govern the language of faith,
how you can use those rules to speak
faith, and as a result, see the windows
of heaven open up on your behalf.

OTHER BOOKS BY
MIKE KEYES SR

Hope The Power to Believe Until You Receive!
ISBN: 978-1-939570-01-7

Have your hopes faded? Are you on the brink of compromise or defeat? Have you been crushed and believe there is no hope? REJOICE! THIS BOOK IS FOR YOU! As long as you're alive and can make a decision, THERE IS HOPE hope for recovery, restoration, and replenishment. Hope stirs nations to action. It keeps people sustained against unbelievable odds. Hope is God's agent of change. It brings joy in times of sorrow, light in times of darkness, and direction when confusion seems to reign. In this crucial teaching, Apostle Mike shares how you can regain hope and claim the victory!

You Can Be Who You Already Are
ISBN: 978-1-949106-11-4

This book is written with a sense of urgency unlike any other the author has written. You Can Be Who You Already Are has at its main core the purpose of helping believers fearlessly rise up in the midst of all the chaos around us and embrace the tremendous opportunities we have to win souls for Jesus in the last days. Many points or verses are repeated for emphasis to help us really grasp the truths presented through the repetition of certain passages, stories or examples found in scripture. You will be enlightened, reminded and encouraged to be who you already are in Christ. You can be the StrongerMan, members of God's congregation of the mighty. You can be who you already are!